I will never become a Christian
a Christian

Seven reasons challenged

DayOne

© Day One Publications 2006

First printed 2006, reprinted 2008

(This is a revised and modernized edition of *I will never become a Christian*, originally published by Bryntirion Press, Wales.)

ISBN 978-1-84625-026-2

9 781846 250262 >

British Library Cataloguing in Publication Data available

Published by Day One Publications

Ryelands Road, Leominster, HR6 8NZ

Telephone 01568 613 740   FAX 01568 611 473

email—sales@dayone.co.uk

web site—www.dayone.co.uk

Designed by Steve Devane and printed by Gutenberg Press, Malta.

I WILL NEVER BECOME **A CHRISTIAN**

CONTENTS

INTRODUCTION

'I will never become a Christian!' I can vividly remember saying this on the morning of 21 May 1955: before the day was out I had done that very thing. I had become a Christian! This book is written for those who are still determined never to become Christians. What you need to realize is that all Christians were once non-Christians, because no one is born a Christian. What is more, very many Christians were just as determined as you never to become Christians. So your position is not unique, nor necessarily unchangeable.

The purpose of this book is twofold: firstly to examine the thinking behind such a resolute avowal not to become a Christian, and secondly to suggest that this is a wholly unreasonable attitude without first examining thoroughly what it means to be a Christian.
Peter Jeffery

1 I WILL NEVER BECOME A CHRISTIAN

People give many reasons for not becoming Christians. Here are some of the more familiar ones.

● All Christians are hypocrites

'All Christians' would include a very large number of people. Therefore, to say that millions of people are hypocrites is to make a statement that is virtually impossible to substantiate. It would be much more accurate to say that some who profess to be Christians are hypocrites. No one would deny that many who go to church on Sunday live their lives for the rest of the week in total disregard of any Christian principles. That is not hypocrisy. It is even worse, because it betrays a complete failure to understand what Christianity is. These people have reduced the living, vibrant faith that is revealed in the New Testament to nothing more than attendance at a church for an hour or so each week.

Neither would we deny that there are people who claim to be Christians, and claim to live by Christian standards, yet who appear to be so devoid of love and compassion that their lives deny what their lips profess. *That* is hypocrisy, and Jesus had great trouble with such people. He opposed them and told them plainly, 'You are like whitewashed tombs, which look beautiful on the outside but on the inside are full of dead men's bones and everything unclean. In the same way, on the outside you appear to people as righteous but on the inside you are full of hypocrisy and wickedness' (*Matthew* 23:27–28).

Christianity has always been plagued with such people. But what does that prove? It does not prove that Christianity is false; rather it proves that Christianity is something that people admire and see as valuable and praiseworthy, even though they themselves fail miserably to achieve its standards. The hypocrite does not pretend to be worse than he or she is, but better. He or she pretends to adhere to Christian standards because they demonstrate a life that is better than the normal.

It is true that many who profess to be Christians are hypocrites, but it is not true that all Christians are hypocrites. There are very many genuine Christians who seek to live their lives by the standard of Jesus. Sometimes they fail and very often fall short of the standard they would like to attain. That is not hypocrisy for the very reason that these Christians are the first to acknowledge their failures. Christians are not perfect and do not claim to be.

To dismiss all Christians as hypocrites is to fly in the face of overwhelming evidence. Think of the immense benefits Christians have brought to mankind. In past years it was evangelical Christians who mobilized opinion and sought to put right many social injustices. William Wilberforce (1759–1833) organized Christian and political opinion in Britain to secure the abolition of slavery. John

Howard (1726–90) pioneered prison reforms, and these were carried out by another Christian, Elizabeth Fry (1780–1845), in London. In Germany Theodore Fliedner (1800–64) was doing a similar work including building hospitals and training nurses. Henri Dunant (1828–1910) founded the Red Cross, while Dr Thomas Barnardo (1845–1905) established children's homes. All these were Christians. Were they hypocrites? Consider the judgement of a famous British statesman included in these words:

Great Britain was the first of the countries of the world to be industrialized, and its workers were caught in a tread-mill of competitive drudgery which kept them straining full sixteen hours a day. Evangelical leaders, including Shaftesbury and members of the Clapham Sect, brought about an end to much of the sorry exploitation and promoted all sorts of social improvements. No less an authority than Prime Minister Lloyd George credited to the Evangelical Revival the movement 'which improved the condition of the working classes in wages, hours of labour and otherwise'. *J. Edwin Orr*

It is easy to make a general statement that all Christians are hypocrites, and it is not difficult to find a few examples to satisfy your conscience. But is it a correct or honest statement? Are you prepared to face up to the real facts? Such a statement appears to be more an emotional reaction than a considered opinion. Emotional reactions tend to spring from ignorance of the facts, or are the result of selecting facts that suit one's case. For instance, a person brought up by a very religious father who went to church regularly and perhaps was even a deacon, but who was a terrible husband and a worse father, might say with great feeling, 'All Christians are hypocrites.' This would be very understandable but it would not be logical. Such a son may as well say that all fathers are hypocrites, or such a daughter that all men are hypocrites. It is an emotional reaction to a particular experience, but it would be totally wrong to generalize from that.

To find one genuine Christian would seriously challenge such a statement. To find ten would destroy it. To find a thousand would be to expose the absurdity of it. Anyone who really wanted to could find one genuine Christian, and it would not be difficult to find ten. To find a thousand in one locality would be difficult but not impossible. The point is that a considered opinion would never lead to the conclusion that all Christians are hypocrites.

I WILL NEVER BECOME A CHRISTIAN BECAUSE ...

● To do so would be to commit intellectual suicide

This viewpoint assumes that Christianity is so lacking in factual evidence and credibility that no sensible, thinking person could possibly believe it. Statements such as 'Science has clearly disproved Christianity and the Bible' usually accompany the 'intellectual suicide' argument. On the basis of such an argument people resolve never to become Christians. Our purpose here is not to prove Christianity and the Bible to be true, but just to show that this argument is not valid.

By implication this comment declares that all Christians have committed intellectual suicide. They are naive, gullible people, who are not prepared to think for themselves. This would have to include Christians like Johannes Kepler (1571–1630). Routes for space travel today are based on his three laws of planetary motion. He wrote, 'Let my name perish if only the name of God the Father is thereby elevated.'

To Kepler's we might add the names of many other distinguished men of science. Michael Faraday (1791–1867), regarded as one of the greatest physicists of all time, was a regular preacher of the gospel. Sir James Young Simpson (1811–70), the discoverer of chloroform, declared at a public meeting that the greatest discovery he ever made was 'that I have a Saviour'. James Clark Maxwell (1831–79) won this tribute from no less a figure than Albert Einstein. Einstein said that Maxwell's work was 'the most profound and most fruitful that physics has experienced since the time of Newton'. Maxwell maintained to the end of his life a firm faith in the truth of the Bible. Sir John Ambrose Fleming (1849–1945), the inventor of the radio valve, said,

There is abundant evidence that the Bible, though written by man, is not the product of the human mind. By countless multitudes it has always been revered as a communication to us from the Creator of the Universe.

Of the scientists of the present time, Professor R.L.F. Boyd, the Head of the Mullard Space Science Laboratory, said, 'I think it is quite as common to find Christians among scientists as in any other profession.'

It is true that for every one scientist who is a Christian, there would be dozens who are not. But that is true of any profession. Intellectual ability, whether a man is a top physicist or a road sweeper, has nothing to do with being a Christian. The fact is that a person can have the highest intellect imaginable and it in no way conflicts with his or her Christian faith. We most certainly do not have to commit intellectual suicide to believe in Christ, or to believe the truth of the Bible.

How reliable is Scripture? This is a fair and crucial question because Christianity stands or falls with the truth or otherwise of the Bible. Is the Bible full of myths or does it contain the truth, the unvarnished truth, about man and God?

We need firstly to understand that the Bible is not one book but a collection of sixty-six books written by about forty people over a period of 1500 years. These writers used their own style and vocabulary, yet the Bible itself claims to be inspired by God. It is God's Word. This is not the wild claim of fanatics but a sober assertion that has much evidence to support it.

What evidence? Consider the fact that over the centuries historians, scientists, religionists and politicians have expended great energy to discredit and destroy the Bible. Why do this if it is just a collection of myths? For centuries the Roman Catholic Church forbad its members to read the Bible, and communist governments did the same thing in the 20th century. Yet the Bible has survived.

Historians and scientists have sought to expose so-called inaccuracies in the Bible; yet sooner or later each 'exposure' is itself exposed as false. For instance, it was asserted that Moses could not have written any part of the Bible as Jesus said he did, because writing was not in existence at the time of Moses. In 1974 and 1975 archaeologists discovered the libraries of the ancient Syrian city of

Ebla. These libraries contained thousands of clay writing-tablets that went back about 800 years before Moses.

It could be objected that because the Bible is an ancient book started 3500 years ago and concluded 2000 years ago, we cannot be sure that what we have today is true to the original. Surely those who copied the copies of the copies etc. must have made mistakes. That would seem reasonable, but consider for a moment how the copies of the ancient Scriptures were made. They were produced by men called scribes and they were amazingly meticulous in checking and correcting their work:

After the scribe finished copying a particular book, he would count all the words and letters it contained. Then he checked this tally against the count for the manuscript that he was copying. He counted the number of times a particular word occurred in the book, and he noted the middle word and the middle letter of the book, comparing all of these with his original. By making these careful checks, he hoped to avoid any scribal errors. *Marshall's Bible Handbook*

What other historical document could boast of such checks and counterchecks?

What about the Bible and science? Surely science has disproved the Bible? The simple answer to that is no. Science has not disproved the Bible because it cannot. For instance, scientists cannot prove that the Genesis account of creation is wrong and evolution is correct. They may give their opinion that they believe one to be wrong and the other correct, but they cannot prove their theory because it is unprovable. Science proves things by actual demonstration, by experiment in a laboratory. If a theory cannot be experimentally demonstrated then it is only hypothesis. As one scientist has said:

All we can do is observe the universe, study its arrangement, behaviour, and laws, and come to the most reasonable conclusion, which would be *consistent* with the facts of science as we know them, as to its ultimate cause and origin. Both evolution and creation are ultimately theories which must be accepted on *faith*. The issue is this: which faith or theory of origins is most reasonable and most consistent with the scientific evidence? *B.G. Ranganathan*

The alleged facts of science are always changing. What scientists believed to be great discoveries of truth and fact fifty years ago, are now discarded for new truths and new facts. Science is not without its difficulties and contradictions. When considering the complexity of the human eye even Charles Darwin had to admit:

To suppose that the eye with all its inimitable contrivances for adjusting the focus to different distances, for admitting different amounts of light, and for the correction of spherical and chromatic aberration, could have been formed by natural selection seems, I freely confess, absurd in the highest degree.

Ranganathan shows how the second law of thermodynamics contradicts other scientific 'facts':

The universally accepted Second Law of Thermodynamics has also been shown to contradict the theory of evolution. This Law simply states that the natural tendency of all things, living or non-living, is toward greater randomness or disorder, rather than greater complexity or organization. For example, if an apple is left on a lawn it will naturally break down and decay to simpler elements rather than evolve into something more complex. Similarly, if a car is left unmaintained, it will naturally rust and deteriorate rather than improve and become structurally more organized. Evolution, however, teaches just the opposite, that simple things naturally become more and more complex ... Furthermore, the commonly accepted theory that our universe, with its highly organized clusters of galaxies, each galaxy containing precise and orderly courses of hundreds of billions of stars, is the result of a random and chaotic explosion, popularly known as the 'Big Bang', is contradictory to and inconsistent with the Second Law of Thermodynamics. The scientific *fact* is that all physical processes in the universe go from order to disorder, *not* from disorder to order.

Science has a very valuable part to play in modern life, but be careful that you do not make it into a religion and worship today what will be inevitably rejected in the near future. Has science disproved the Bible? *Time* magazine once ran a cover story on the Bible. This was its conclusion:

The breadth, sophistication and diversity of all this biblical investigation are impressive, but it begs a question: Has it made the Bible more credible or less? Literalists who feel the ground move when a verse is challenged would have to say that credibility has suffered. Doubt has been sown, faith is in jeopardy. But believers who expect something else from the Bible may well conclude that its credibility has been enhanced. After more than two centuries of facing the heaviest scientific guns that could be brought to bear, the Bible has survived—and is perhaps the better for the siege. Even on the critics' own terms—historical fact—the Scriptures seem more acceptable now than they did when the rationalists began the attack.

No Christian need be embarrassed by what he or she believes. The intellectual suicide argument is shown to have no real substance when one reads statements like that of Professor T.L. More, a very vocal evolutionist. 'The more one studies paleontology [the fossil record], the more certain one becomes that evolution is based on faith *alone.'*

Other statements from famous evolutionists are to the same effect. Professor D.M.S. Watson writes, 'Evolution itself is accepted by zoologists, not because it has been observed to occur or can be proved by logically coherent evidence, but because the only alternative—special creation—is clearly incredible.' Again Sir Arthur Keith says, 'Evolution is unproved and unprovable. We believe it only because the only alternative is special creation which is unthinkable.' From this one is tempted to conclude that it is not the Christians who should be charged with violence against the intellect! Surely Professor Edwin Conklin of Princeton University was right when he stated: 'The probability of life originating from accident is comparable to the probability of the unabridged dictionary resulting from an explosion in a printing shop.'

● **Christianity is just a crutch for those who cannot face up to reality: it is 'pie in the sky when you die'!**

It is certainly true that there are millions of people who cannot face up to the realities of life. That is why so many turn to drink and drugs to escape reality. That is why so many marriages end in divorce. That is why so many hospital beds are filled with people suffering from depression and mental illnesses.

Most people have a crutch of some sort to support them in the turmoil of modern living. Work, sport, money can all become a crutch without which life cannot be faced. But a crutch is for the sick not the healthy, for the weak not the strong. Christianity is not a crutch; on the contrary it kicks the crutch away and allows a man to stand strong. Christianity exposes the sickness and deals with it. In becoming a Christian a man does not take hold of a crutch; rather he throws away the crutch that has been supporting him for years.

The record of Christianity in this matter is impressive. Lives have been transformed. Drunkards, prostitutes, thieves have all been changed. Drug addicts have found a new meaning to life.

A remarkable illustration of this is found in the life of the American preacher Dr Harry Ironside (1876–1951). One Sunday he was speaking at an open-air meeting in San Francisco. When he finished one of the listening crowd gave him a card. On one side was a name that Ironside recognized immediately. The man was well known for his anti-Christian views. As Ironside turned the card over he read, 'Sir, I challenge you to debate with me the question,

Agnosticism versus Christianity, in the Academy of Science Hall next Sunday afternoon at four o'clock. I will pay all expenses.'

Ironside accepted the challenge but on the condition that his opponent should bring with him two people whose qualifications proved that agnosticism was of real value in changing lives and building character. He was to find a man and woman whose lives had been rotten; ruined by drugs, or drink, or crime, or prostitution. They were to be people who, having heard Christianity denounced and agnosticism advocated, had vowed they too would become agnostics. The new power which had thus come into their lives would have enabled them to break with the old habits and to become new people. Said Ironside, 'If you promise to bring two people like that, I will bring a hundred who lived a similar sort of life but who have been gloriously changed by the power of the Lord Jesus Christ.'

The invitation to debate was withdrawn.

Most Christians could tell you of the various crutches that propped up their lives before they became Christians, but which they no longer need. They have Jesus, the Rock, on whom to build their lives. Have you, who are determined never to become a Christian, truly faced up to the realities of life and recognized the crutches you need to keep you going?

I WILL NEVER BECOME A CHRISTIAN BECAUSE ...

● **There's nothing special about Christianity!**
The world is full of religions, and isn't one as good as the other so long as you are sincere? Don't all the different religions lead to God?

Are we not all the children of God? You may not like the answer to these questions, but the fact is that Christianity is very special.

All religions are *not* the same, and all do *not* lead to God, and we are *not* all children of God. To many that may sound intolerant and bigoted, but really it is most reasonable and logical.

It has been said that man is incurably religious. He must have something to worship. There is something in his nature that compels him to this. Through the centuries man has continually invented gods and religions, and today the situation is exactly the same as far as the traditional religions are concerned. Nowadays, however, the gods may take the form of a pop star, a sport, a car, etc. instead of the old-fashioned idols, but the motive and desire are the same. Many who follow pop music or sport would probably say that it was not a religion, and that they were not religious. That may be true of the casual fan, but of the ardent supporter it is not true. The devotion shown, the time given and the money spent can be described only in terms of religious fervour.

People want a religion but they do not want God. Hence they invent religions and systems of worship that exclude the one true and living God. A person may be very genuine and sincere in his or her religious observance; but it is not a matter of sincerity, it is a matter of truth. It is possible to be sincerely wrong.

Christianity is special because it was not invented by man. Christianity is God coming to us in the person of his Son, the Lord Jesus Christ. It is so special that Jesus said, 'I am the way and the truth and the life. No one comes to the Father except through me' (John 14:6). It is so special that in one of the first Christian sermons ever preached, the apostle Peter could say about Jesus, 'Salvation is found in no one else, for there is no other name under heaven given to men by which we must be saved' (*Acts* 4:12).

Those two statements reveal the uniqueness and exclusiveness of the Christian faith. That is why you and everyone else need to become Christians. We are not all the children of God. That is a common belief that has no substance in fact. Jesus once said to a group of people who thought themselves to be very respectable and moral and religious, 'You belong to your father, the devil ... you do not belong to God' (*John* 8:44,47).

Is it reasonable to believe that all religions lead to God when they so obviously contradict each other? Is it reasonable to believe that all people are children of God when they so obviously ignore him and many even deny he exists? Is it not reasonable to believe that if there is a God who loves us, then he will not leave us groping in spiritual darkness but come to us with light and truth? And if God is to do this, would he not do it clearly? Christians believe God has done this and that Jesus is the light and truth we need. He alone is the way to God.

Christianity is much more than mere religion. Religion is man groping after God, whereas in the Lord Jesus Christ God reveals himself to man. The difference between man's religion and biblical Christianity is that Christianity faces up honestly to what man is and who God is. Human nature is not essentially good; it is sinful. It is in rebellion against the holy God. This is why religion with its moral cosmetics always fails. Religion is man papering over the cracks in the walls, when the building's foundations are collapsing. It is an exercise in futility. Christianity is God's answer to human sin and as such it is the only answer.

I WILL NEVER BECOME A CHRISTIAN BECAUSE …

● Christians cannot even agree among themselves!

The confusion that gives rise to this objection is very understandable. The non-Christian listening to all the different voices claiming to be Christian must be thoroughly bewildered. They cannot all be right, so which, if any, is? To whom are we to listen: the Pope, or the Archbishop of Canterbury, or Billy Graham, the well-known American evangelist? How can we know the truth?

It should not be too surprising that the confusion exists. Anything of true value is sure at some time to be counterfeited. That is exactly what confronts us in this problem. There is much that goes under the name of Christianity, and though it bears a resemblance to the genuine it is nothing but a counterfeit. This has been the situation for nearly 2000 years, but it has not prevented millions from becoming Christians.

So how do we tell the true from the false?

Because Christians are human beings and not programmed computers, it is inevitable that they will not all agree on everything. True Christians do disagree on many secondary issues, but on the essential matters they all agree. This is evident from the great historical confessions of faith produced by Anglicans, Baptists, Presbyterians and other bodies. There are differences, but not on essential questions such as who is Jesus? what about the resurrection? how do we become Christians? etc.

The disagreements that are the probable cause of confusion are not minor. When a so-called Christian bishop or church leader says that Jesus is not God, and another says he is, both cannot be right. That matter is not incidental but crucial and you cannot reconcile such opposite views. If one voice says Jesus rose from the dead literally and physically, and another denies it, then one must be wrong.

Which is the authentic voice of Christianity and which is the counterfeit? That dilemma can be resolved by starting with a simple and most reasonable premise. A true Christian will take the teaching of Christ seriously. When Jesus says that in order to be a Christian you must be born again, there can be no argument. When Jesus teaches that there is a terrible place called hell, then whether we like it or not, all Christians will believe it.

What value would there be in following a Jesus whose teaching has to be constantly changed, adapted, and reinterpreted? The true Christian simply takes Jesus seriously and follows the teaching he gave us either directly or through his apostles. For these Christians, the New Testament is to be believed and taught. They do not apologize for it and are not embarrassed by it.

Whom shall we believe? Believe Jesus Christ. God said, 'Listen to him!' (*Matthew* 17:5).

<u>I WILL NEVER BECOME A CHRISTIAN BECAUSE ...</u>

● A God of love could not possibly allow all the evil and suffering there is in the world!

The problem this objection raises is a very real one because evil and suffering are all around us. We experience pain, sickness and death, and we all see on our TVs pictures of famine and earthquake. The question inevitably is, Why does this happen? The tendency then is for many to blame God. They may never thank God for all the goodness, kindness, and beauty there are in the world, but they blame God for all the bad features.

Of course, this is not true of everyone. When evil and suffering touch them personally there are some people who, in their anguish and pain, may well ask why. But they do not blame God. Instead they find great comfort in knowing that God does love them and care deeply for them in their trials.

Some years ago, a family was leaving church after the Sunday evening service. The father crossed the road to return the chapel key, while the mother and two children, Christopher aged nine and Susan aged four and a half, waited on the pavement. The road had three lanes, and down the middle lane two cars came speeding towards each other. Neither driver took evasive action, and the result was a crash, with one car sent hurtling across the road into the waiting family. Both children were killed and the mother sustained injuries which kept her on crutches for many weeks.

How would you cope in a situation like that? Relating her feelings at the time, the mother said,

How people who have no faith in God manage in a time of crisis I do not know. We prayed there at the roadside amid all the confusion. How wonderful our heavenly Father is! He is always at hand.

This is no escapism and refusal to face the facts. The pain and heartache for those parents were very real, and still are many years later. The father said,

Looking back over the past years, it is still difficult for us to understand why the Lord allowed this event in our lives which brought us so much heartache, but his grace is sufficient for the greatest needs.

This incident shows us that disaster and adversity, in and of themselves, are no reason to reject God and the Christian faith. The judge in the subsequent trial did not blame God. With all the facts and evidence before him, he blamed the drivers: 'I have no doubt that this was, on the part of each of you, a disgraceful piece of driving.' Surely it is a fact beyond question that much of the suffering in the world is the result of man's greed, selfishness, and rejection of God's way. Millions of people are starving in Africa, but in western Europe farmers have to work to quotas and are not allowed to produce as much food as their land is capable of doing. The reason given is that it is not economic, and we even hear of perfectly good food being destroyed for the same economic reason. A decade ago it was reported that it would take seventeen billion American dollars a year to feed all the hungry people in the world. That may seem an immense amount of money, but it was only what some big nations were spending every two weeks on armaments at that time. Famine is not the cause of hunger in the world; rather it is man's greed and selfishness.

You may concede that, but what about earthquakes, tsunamis, hurricanes, and floods? Man cannot be blamed for those. If God is so good and so powerful, why does he not do something about all this suffering? The answer is that he *has* done something.

When God made this world, none of these evils had a place. God looked at his creation and it was very good—there were not even weeds, let alone earthquakes. Man himself was made in the image of God. He was not made as a robot programmed to act in a prescribed way, but as a free agent to enjoy all that God gave him in a beautiful world. So far so good. No evil and no suffering. Then man rebelled against God and sin became a part of man's nature. Under the influence of the devil man rejects God and all God's ways. The rejection is so complete that even Jesus describes Satan as the 'prince of this world' (*John* 14:30). The result of all this is the world in which we now live. There is still much of the beauty of God's handiwork to be seen, but we also see all the evil of sin, not only in man's nature but also in creation itself, so that the New Testament describes creation as 'groaning as in the pains of childbirth' (*Romans* 8:22).

The world as we know it is not the harmonious structure that came fresh from the hand of God, and over which the refrain was repeated 'it was good'. Instead there is a discord which has affected the fabric of creation, the functioning of nature, and the pattern of animal and human life. So we have savage and destructive elements in nature which manifest themselves in earthquake and flood. We have nature 'red in tooth and claw' with one species preying upon another. We have malarial mosquitoes and disease-carrying germs. We have, in short, a creation in a state of deep discord, and the consequences of that discord reverberate in every corner of life. *Herbert Carson*

That is the Bible's account of the world and life as we know it today. It fits the facts; it explains our experiences; and more than that—it goes on to provide an answer to our question. God has done something about suffering. He sent Jesus his Son into the world to defeat sin and Satan, to save man from the consequence of his sin, and ultimately in his good time to produce a new heaven and a new earth, where everything will be exactly as God meant it to be. Once more there will be no evil, no sin, and no suffering.

The Old Testament prophet Isaiah describes it like this:

The wolf will live with the lamb, the leopard will lie down with the goat, the calf and the lion and the yearling together; and a little child will lead them. The cow will feed with the bear, their young will lie down together, and the lion will eat straw like the ox. The infant will play near the hole of the cobra, and the young child put his hand into the viper's nest. They will neither harm nor destroy on all my holy mountain, for the earth will be full of the knowledge of the Lord as the waters cover the sea (11:6–9).

It is because those parents involved in that awful accident believed this that the outrage and calamity they suffered did not embitter them against God. Rather they were given strength and hope in the midst of very real pain and anguish.

I WILL NEVER BECOME A CHRISTIAN BECAUSE ...

● Religion, including Christianity, has been responsible for a good deal of trouble in the world!

Religious tension and fighting, such as between Muslims and Christians in Bosnia or Protestants and Catholics in Northern Ireland, are not a good advertisement for Christianity. Most Christians cringe when they see reports of such things on TV. They cringe, not in embarrassment and shame at the antics of fellow believers, but because the name of their Saviour is blatantly abused by some political cause that bears not the slightest relationship to the life and teaching of the Lord Jesus Christ.

Most people inherit their religion by an accident of birth. If you were born in Spain it is very probable that you would be a Roman Catholic. If you were born in England it is likely you would be a Protestant. If you were born in Pakistan you would probably be a Muslim. The problem with this sort of thing is that the religion becomes more of a patriotic or political tag than a spiritual experience. God has very little, if any, part in the life of a person whose religion comes from this source. How often do you think that those who did the killing in Ireland under the name of Protestant or Catholic ever entered a church to worship?

It is true that in history the Crusades and the Spanish Inquisition sought to justify themselves in the name of Christianity. However, none of these wars then, and such wars now, were or are spiritually motivated. In them all there are major and extreme political or nationalistic tendencies. If there was no such thing as a Bible, the horrors associated with them would still have been perpetrated. Religion becomes the excuse for them, not the reason. All these things reveal clearly how totally unsatisfactory is an inherited religion. It does not matter what the religion is, if it is merely a tag we have because of an accident of birth it will cause us more harm than good. It is possible to inherit a religion, but it is not possible to inherit a true, living faith in God. Faith is a personal experience, and when a person truly knows God as he has revealed himself in Jesus, he or she does not plot to kill but prays for others to know the eternal life which is the gift of God.

In the UK in recent years it has been thrilling to hear of former IRA and Loyalist terrorists who have come to a true faith in the Lord Jesus Christ. One of these men described what motivated his actions as a terrorist:

Animated by deep patriotical commitment to the cause of liberating our still occupied and truncated province from the hand of the imperial coloniser, I with others conspired to make a bomb with the intention of inflicting injury and death on those who denied us our national identity.

You can see there is not the slightest hint of anything religious in that. It is totally political and nationalistic extremism and is probably typical of all such terrorists. The same man went on to describe how God dealt with him in mercy and grace:

I was aware most terribly of my lostness and my filthiness in his sight, yet even more aware of the remedy. I hated my past life with a desire only for the freedom which the Son of Man brings. I was not aware of a choice, only of a necessity. I prayed, 'Lord Jesus, I know that you died for me, please come into my life and make me what you want me to be.' All the questions melted away as the Answer came in! Thus did I pass from death to life.

From this example perhaps we can learn that, far from being the cause of fighting and killing, true, biblical Christianity is the only answer as it changes the hearts of men and women and gives them a purpose far higher than anything political or nationalistic can.

We have considered objections as to why some folk are determined never to become Christians. Let us finally consider an objection that is rarely voiced but perhaps lies behind many of the others.

I WILL NEVER BECOME A CHRISTIAN BECAUSE ...

● **I am afraid—afraid of what friends and family will say; afraid of what I will have to give up; afraid that I will never be able to keep it up!**
Such fears are not uncommon, and from the standpoint of the person feeling them they are not unreasonable. It is a fact that if you become a Christian, some friends will not understand—they may think that you have 'gone all religious' and make fun of you. It is a fact that if you become a Christian, then certain things in your life are going to have to change. It is a fact that if you become a Christian it will not be easy, and left to yourself you will not be able to keep it up.

I suppose that most Christians felt like this at first, but we soon found that the amazing grace of God sustained us. This fact far outweighs the rest. We discovered that it was more important what God thought of us than what friends thought. Eventually the friends stopped making fun and accepted us as we were. We discovered that what we received in Christ was far more valuable than anything we gave up. It was not so much giving things up as having better things edging them out. We discovered also that it was not so much a question of our keeping it up, but of God's keeping us up.

No one ever regrets becoming a real Christian. Read the testimonies at the end of this book and you will see that this is true.

2 WHAT IS A CHRISTIAN?

To say that you will never become a Christian is totally
unreasonable unless you have first given serious thought
to what Christianity is. For instance, have you ever read the
New Testament? Have you considered the person called
Jesus Christ? You cannot reject what you do not know.

The Christian faith rests firmly on the teaching of the Bible, so
consider now what this teaching is.

WHAT THE BIBLE SAYS ABOUT …

● Man

'There is no one who does good, not even one' (*Romans* 3:12).
'All have sinned and fall short of the glory of God' (*Romans* 3:23).

'As for you, you were dead in your transgressions and sins, in which you
used to live when you followed the ways of this world and of the ruler of
the kingdom of the air, the spirit who is now at work in those who are
disobedient. All of us also lived among them at one time, gratifying the
cravings of our sinful nature and following its desires and thoughts. Like
the rest, we were by nature objects of wrath' (*Ephesians* 2:1–3).

'For out of the heart come evil thoughts, murder, adultery, sexual immorality, theft, false testimony, slander' (*Matthew* 15:19).

'If we claim to be without sin, we deceive ourselves and the truth is not in us' (*1 John* 1:8).

● Sin

'All wrongdoing is sin' (*1 John* 5:17).

'Everyone who sins breaks the law; in fact, sin is lawlessness' (*1 John* 3:4).

● The consequences of sin

'Your iniquities have separated you from your God; your sins have hidden his face from you, so that he will not hear' (*Isaiah* 59:2).

'For the wages of sin is death' (*Romans* 6:23).

● Jesus

'The virgin will be with child and will give birth to a son, and will call him Immanuel' (*Isaiah* 7:14; *Matthew* 1:22–23).

'The Son is the radiance of God's glory and the exact representation of his being' (*Hebrews* 1:3).

'He is the image of the invisible God' (*Colossians* 1:15).

'For God was pleased to have all his fulness dwell in him' (*Colossians* 1:19).

'The Son of Man did not come to be served, but to serve, and to give his life as a ransom for many' (*Mark* 10:45).

'But God demonstrates his own love for us in this: While we were still sinners, Christ died for us' (*Romans* 5:8).

'He himself bore our sins in his body on the tree, so that we might die to sins and live for righteousness; by his wounds you have been healed' (*1 Peter* 2:24).

'For Christ died for sins once for all, the righteous for the unrighteous, to bring you to God' (*1 Peter* 3:18).

● Salvation

'Jesus answered, "I am the way and the truth and the life. No one comes to the Father except through me'" (*John* 14:6).

'Salvation is found in no one else, for there is no other name under heaven given to men by which we must be saved' (*Acts* 4:12).

'For it is by grace you have been saved, through faith—and this not from yourselves, it is the gift of God—not by works, so that no one can boast' (*Ephesians* 2:8–9).

'But when the kindness and love of God our Saviour appeared, he saved us, not because of righteous things we had done, but because of his mercy' (*Titus* 3:4).

'"What must I do to be saved?" They replied, "Believe in the Lord Jesus, and you will be saved"' (*Acts* 16:30–31).

'If you confess with your mouth, "Jesus is Lord," and believe in your heart that God raised him from the dead, you will be saved' (*Romans* 10:9).

● Man's response

'He commands all people everywhere to repent' (*Acts* 17:30).

'If we confess our sins, he is faithful and just and will forgive us our sins' (*1 John* 1:9).

'When the people heard this, they were cut to the heart and said to Peter and the other apostles, "Brothers, what shall we do?" Peter replied, "Repent and be baptised, everyone of you, in the name of Jesus Christ so that your sins may be forgiven"' (*Acts* 2:37–38).

'This is the verdict: Light has come into the world, but men loved darkness instead of light because their deeds were evil. Everyone who does evil hates the light, and will not come into the light for fear that his deeds will be exposed' (*John* 3:19–20).

● Those who do not believe and repent

'Whoever rejects the Son will not see life, for God's wrath remains on him' (*John* 3:36).

'Man is destined to die once, and after that to face judgement' (*Hebrews* 9:27).

'They will be punished with everlasting destruction and shut out from the presence of the Lord' (*2 Thessalonians* 1:9).

● Those who believe and repent

'I tell you the truth, whoever hears my word and believes him who sent me has eternal life and will not be condemned; he has crossed over from death to life' (*John* 5:24).

'To all who received him, to those who believed in his name, he gave the right to become children of God' (*John* 1:12).

'Therefore, if anyone is in Christ, he is a new creation; the old has gone, the new has come!' (2 *Corinthians* 5:17).

'Therefore, since we have been justified through faith, we have peace with God through our Lord Jesus Christ' (*Romans* 5:1).

These are not verses wrenched out of their context to justify a particular viewpoint, as you will see if you read the context. This is the consistent teaching of the Bible about the most crucial issues that face man.

All the problems of the world—poverty, war, AIDS—can be traced eventually to what man is. Man is not essentially good and evolving gradually to perfection. The facts of history and man's present behaviour deny that. Man is, as described in the Bible, a sinner in rebellion against God, and our history proves that. Man behaves as he does because he has rejected God. Therefore the answers to man's problems are not political or social; they are spiritual. Man needs God, and the only way he will find God is through the Lord Jesus Christ.

That, basically, is the claim of biblical Christianity. Note, *biblical* Christianity—not institutionalized, formal Christianity, but the Christianity that unashamedly takes its stand on the teaching of the Bible.

If you say you will never become a Christian, you should at least understand what a Christian is. Would it surprise you to know that the word 'Christian' is found in the Bible only three times? In other words, it is used sparingly and not bandied about as, unfortunately, it is today. Consequently there are many popular misconceptions as to what a Christian is. Let us consider some of these.

ANYONE WHO GOES TO CHURCH IS A CHRISTIAN

It is true that Christians will go to church, and they will have little tolerance for the nonsense that says you can be a good Christian and never go to church. Of course there are Christians who, because of ill-health, cannot attend church. They would go if possible, because they love their church. But going to church in and of itself has never made anyone a Christian. John Wesley, the founder of Methodism, not only went to church but was an ordained minister of the Church of England before he became a Christian.

MY COUNTRY IS A CHRISTIAN COUNTRY, SO ANYONE BORN THERE IS A CHRISTIAN

We have to say firstly, and sadly, that there are many countries that profess to be Christian but are not. That is another example of the misuse of the word 'Christian'. Even if the UK, for example, were a Christian country, simply being born here could not make a person a Christian. The same is true about being born into a Christian family. A person's faith and beliefs cannot be inherited. They are personal. The circumstances of background may contribute to what a person believes, but they do not determine it.

Would you consider India a Christian country? Probably not, but almost certainly there are more Christians in India than there are in the UK.

A CHRISTIAN IS SOMEONE WHO LIVES A GOOD MORAL LIFE

Christians will certainly try to live a good moral life, but they also knows that this will not make them Christian. At the same time, there are thousands of people who live good moral lives who make no claim to being Christian. The Bible makes it very clear that the best a person can do is not good enough to make him or her acceptable to God, and a real Christian would not quarrel with the prophet Isaiah when he wrote, 'All our righteous acts are like filthy rags' in the sight of God (64:6).

Putting your trust in these things to make you acceptable to God is like having a counterfeit ticket for a big football match. You buy the ticket in good faith. You happily go along to the ground confident that you will get in, but at the gate there is a terrible shock awaiting you. Your sincerity, your genuineness, your tears of grief will do you no good. You have been deceived and there is no entrance for you.

So then, what is a Christian?

A CHRISTIAN IS SOMEONE WHO KNOWS HE OR SHE IS A SINNER

Of all the words in the Bible, the one which is perhaps the most hated and misunderstood today is the word 'sin'. How often do you hear it mentioned in a religious service on TV or radio? It is not unusual for preachers to be criticized if they say people in the congregation are sinners. 'We are not sinners, we are respectable people', is the protest.

Do you see the problem this creates? There are two definitions of a sinner. The first says a sinner is someone who is a thief, or a murderer, or a drunk, or a drug addict. The other definition, which you find in the Bible, says we are all sinners. The problem is a major one for it is not merely a matter of defining a word. Our whole attitude to God is involved. What, then, is sin? What is a sinner?

We must first distinguish between 'sin' and 'sins'. In the above paragraph the deficiency of the first definition of 'sinner' is that it talks about particular sins, leading to the conclusion that if I am not guilty of those I am not a sinner. This is wrong. Sins are merely the fruit of a root condition in the human heart called sin.

In other words it is not that we are sinners because we commit sins, but that we commit sins because we are sinners. It is not the wrong things we do that make us sinners. Rather we do the wrong things because sin is part of our human nature.

The Bible teaches very clearly that we are all sinners by nature. Therefore, the root problem is our sinful hearts, and our sinful actions are the inevitable fruit of this. That is why the Bible says, 'There is no difference, for all have sinned' (*Romans* 3:22–23). There may well be a difference in one man's actions and behaviour from those of another—that is in his *sins*. With regard to his *sin*, to his heart, to what he is by nature, there is no difference. The real problem is not so much what a man does, it is what he is. Drug-pushing, lies, stealing, jealousy, anger, pride are all different sins that come from the same source—man's sinful heart.

Christians are those who have come to know this. There was a time when each of them would have denied it. There was certainly a time when it did not bother them. But it became a matter of real concern. A sense of personal sin and guilt is the first step for anyone becoming a Christian. If we will not face up to the fact of our own sin and guilt and take it seriously we will never become Christians. The reason we do not take sin seriously is that we do not take God seriously. We see him as some sort of policeman that it is possible for us to fool, and therefore we imagine we get away with our sin.

The coach sped down the road carrying its passengers on a day trip to the seaside. The driver chatted to those sitting near the front, pointing out interesting landmarks. After a while it was noticed that the drivers of coaches and lorries coming towards us were giving our driver the thumbs-down sign. He knew what it meant. There was a police radar speed-trap ahead, so he slowed down. Sure enough, we soon saw a policeman standing at the roadside with a radar-gun in his hand. We passed him well within the speed limit, and as soon as we passed our speed increased and our driver began to give the thumbs-down sign to lorries and coaches coming towards us. The policeman would not have caught many law-breakers that day! The law was politely observed for only as long as was necessary. In effect, the law enforcer was an object of scorn.

There is a law and a law enforcer that are not so easily fooled. God's law can be broken a thousand times and we think we have escaped scot-free. The Bible calls breaking God's law sin and declares, 'Be sure that your sin will find you out' (*Numbers* 32:23).

A CHRISTIAN IS SOMEONE WHO KNOWS HE OR SHE CAN DO NOTHING TO DEAL WITH PERSONAL SIN

Turning over a new leaf, pulling yourself up by your boot laces, trying your best, are all the remedies of religion. The Christian probably tried them all at one time or another and found them to be useless in dealing with his sinful nature.

It is true that criminals can reform and give up their life of crime. In other words, they deal with some of their sins, but they are still sinners. Instead of being law-breaking sinners they are now law-abiding sinners. Their natures remain unchanged. In the Old

Testament God puts a very penetrating question to us: 'Can the Ethiopian change his skin or the leopard its spots?' (*Jeremiah* 13:23). The answer is no, and the same applies to man changing his nature. No Christian ever came to believe this quickly or easily. It goes very much against the grain of human pride, but again it is an essential stage in becoming a Christian.

A CHRISTIAN IS SOMEONE WHO BELIEVES THAT THERE IS ONLY ONE ANSWER TO SIN

That is the answer God provides for us. A Christian is a sinner who has been saved by the grace of God from the consequence and power of sin.

There is no bypassing this. To ignore God's requirements is the height of foolishness. Several years ago I was in the departure lounge of Heathrow Airport waiting to board a plane to Australia. Sitting not far from me was a young woman who was obviously in distress. The airline staff kept coming back and forth to her. Questions were being asked and the young woman's distress increased. Eventually she was led away. Apparently her problem was that though she had a valid passport and had purchased a ticket she did not have an entrance visa to Australia. Like everyone else she would have been told that a visa was essential but for some reason she chose to ignore this. Now when the crunch came, with the plane ready to take off, she was not allowed to board.

Australia requires a visa, which it will supply very readily, if anyone is to enter the land. God requires that all our sin be dealt with if we are to enter heaven. This very requirement God himself meets in the

Lord Jesus Christ. Ignore this, and like that young woman at Heathrow there will be no entrance for you.

This is so important that we need to spend some time on it. We will do so by considering the words of Jesus in what is probably the most famous verse in the Bible: 'For God so loved the world that he gave his one and only Son, that whoever believes in him shall not perish but have eternal life' (*John* 3:16).

Jesus speaks of two parties: God and the world. He also tells us a most important thing about these two—God loves, and the world perishes. Consider carefully these two statements.

God loves. What do you make of that? Do you think that that is to be expected? That that is what God is supposed to do? That there is nothing extraordinary in God's loving us? You could not be more wrong! There is nothing more amazing or astonishing than this. Let me prove it to you.

Could you love someone who went around telling lies about you? Someone who blamed you for all his or her troubles, ignored you, denied that you matter, or even existed? That is how the world treats God—and remember, the world is you and millions like you.

Why are we like that? Jesus tells us in verse 19 of the passage—it is because we are sinners. 'This is the verdict: Light has come into the world, but men loved darkness instead of light because their deeds were evil.' What does the word 'verdict' suggest? It suggests that the trial has already taken place; the evidence has been considered and the sentence passed. That is why the world perishes. It is because we are guilty and condemned. 'Perish' means God's holy judgement upon sin. To perish means more than the death of the body. It includes one factor most people never contemplate.

As usual after the evening service the teenagers of the church had gone back to the Pastor's home. When the Pastor arrived later the boys were engrossed in a serious discussion on what was the worst way to die. They had come up with a list of most painful deaths, including being eaten by a crocodile, being run over by a steam-roller, and being boiled in oil. The list was long and gruesome. When the Pastor came in they asked his opinion. He answered them simply: the worst way to die is without Christ.

The means by which any of us die is unimportant compared to the spiritual state in which we are when we die. There are only two spiritual states or conditions: with Christ as our Saviour or without him. The Bible says that there are two deaths. They are the first death and the second death. The first death is the death of the body, and all, Christian or non-Christian, experience this. The second death, which is hell (*Revelation* 20:14), Christians are spared, because their sin, which deserves hell, has been dealt with by their Saviour on the cross of Calvary. That is the clear teaching of Jesus concerning mankind and our relationship to God. Really we are in a terrible situation. Found guilty; verdict declared already; will we perish? what hope is there?

Our only hope is that 'God so loved the world'. God loves those who do not deserve it. Indeed, we would have to acknowledge that far from deserving the love of God, we deserve the exact opposite. But the fact that God loves sinners is not sufficient to remove our condemnation and guilt. God's love must find a way of dealing with our sins. God is holy. He has come to a verdict and the sentence he has pronounced must be carried out. So it still seems hopeless. It appears that God's love is not helping us. But listen to what Jesus goes on to say—'he gave his one and only Son'. What does that mean?

It is a direct reference to the death of Jesus on the cross. The context, especially verses 14 and 15, proves that. Being 'lifted up' refers to the cross. Listen to *John* 12:32 and 33—'"But I, when I am lifted up from the earth, will draw all. men to myself." He said this to show the kind of death he was going to die.' This is the heart of the Christian gospel. This is how God has dealt with our sin.

To explain the meaning of the death of Jesus, let us consider another statement in the New Testament. 'For Christ died for sins once for all, the righteous for the unrighteous, to bring you to God' (*1 Peter* 3:18).

For centuries the cross has been the undisputed symbol of Christianity. By the cross we do not mean a crucifix, which is a symbol of weakness and defeat, but an empty cross, a symbol of strength and victory. The cross is the place where Jesus died, and the death of the Saviour is the key doctrine of Christianity. It is significant that the four Gospel writers in the New Testament, in recording the thirty-three years of the life of Jesus, give almost a third of their space to the last week of his life. Obviously they considered his death and resurrection, together with the events leading up to them, of prime importance.

What, then, is the meaning of the cross? What is the significance for us of the death of Jesus? To answer these questions, we will look at this verse and try to understand what it means. It tells us four things about the death of our Saviour.

● 1. The wonder of it

Christ died. This is the wonder of Calvary. Crucifixion was common enough in the first century. There was nothing unusual about it. The marvel of this crucifixion consists not in the act but the person. *Christ died.*

'Christ' is the English version of a Greek word *Christos*; the Hebrew equivalent is rendered 'Messiah', and the English translation would be 'the Anointed One'. It was a title reserved for a very special person. Another name of the Lord Jesus Christ is Immanuel, which means 'God with us'. Christ is God, and dies on the cross. This is the wonder of it. The Immortal dies.

In the verse which we are examining, Christ is also called 'the righteous'. This is yet another title used for our Saviour in the New Testament (*Acts* 3:14; 7:52; 22:14). It speaks of the purity and sinlessness of Jesus. No action, no word ever came from him that was inconsistent with the requirements of God's law. No thought, no desire dwelt in his mind that was inconsistent with the spirit of God's law. He left this world as he entered it—holy, sinless, undefiled. But the character of Christ was not merely free from sin; it was distinguished with every possible moral excellence—love, mercy, truth, kindness, goodness, compassion.

These two titles tell us the wonder of Calvary. As he was the Righteous One, death had no way of claiming him. Death is the wages of sin, and he had not sinned, he did not deserve to die. As the Christ, the living God, he had power over death, as was demonstrated by the raising of Lazarus, and therefore death could not snatch him away.

Yet Christ, the Righteous One, died. Why?

● 2. The meaning of it

We are told two truths concerning the meaning of Christ's death. It was *for sins.* It was *for the unrighteous.*

It was a punishment for sins, and yet we have already seen that Christ did not sin, so for whose sins was he punished? We are given the answer. He was punished for the sins of the unrighteous. When he died, he was acting on behalf of others. Elsewhere in his Epistle, Peter states this truth very clearly: 'He himself bore our sins in his body on the tree' (2:24). Indeed, this is what the Bible is always repeating: 'He was pierced for our transgressions, he was crushed for our iniquities' (*Isaiah* 53:5). 'Christ died for the ungodly' (Romans 5:6).

These verses declare the great biblical doctrine of the substitutionary death of Jesus to atone for sin. We are all familiar with the idea of a substitute in sport. The team is chosen and another player acts as the sub. If anyone is not playing well or is injured, the substitute comes on and takes his place. This goes part-way to explaining how Jesus is the sinners' substitute. In life we are not performing well; in fact we are making a mess of things. Sin has injured and wounded us, and if we are allowed to carry on in the same vein that sin will condemn us to the wrath of God. Jesus takes upon himself our sin and guilt and faces the wrath of God instead of us. He dies for us on the cross.

What does it all mean at a personal level? It means that my deceit, pride, envy, jealousy, and the rest of my sins, all of which condemn me to hell, Jesus takes upon himself. He takes my guilt and is punished instead of me. This is what the Bible teaches. The atoning death of Jesus is God's answer to sin and, as such, is the only effective answer to human sinfulness and guilt.

Can it really be true? If someone is found guilty in one of our courts and sentenced to twenty years' imprisonment, could someone volunteer to go to prison instead of the guilty one? No. The law of the land requires the guilty, not the innocent, to suffer. In other words, the law does not recognize the punishment of a substitute. With this we all agree. But God does recognize it, and we ought to breathe a huge sigh of relief that it is so.

It is *not* fair that Jesus should die for us. However, strictly speaking, fairness does not enter into it. It is an act of God's love and grace. It is all thoroughly undeserved, and even unexpected. It is not fair, but it is perfectly just. Justice is not perverted, because the sin is punished. When Jesus takes our sin, he takes our guilt as well, and therefore dies as though guilty:

> The enormous load of human guilt
> Was on my Saviour laid;
> With woes as with a garment he
> For sinners was arrayed.
>
> And in the fearful pangs of death
> He wept, he prayed for me;
> Loved and embraced my guilty soul
> When nailéd to the tree.
> *William Williams*

The heart of the matter is this. God is Judge. We are the guilty ones. The Judge does not require the guilty to provide some innocent friend to suffer for them. There are no innocents, for all have sinned. All are guilty. The Judge says, 'I will suffer instead of you. I will pay the price. I will die. I will become man, and as the sinless man, as the innocent Jesus, I will die for guilty sinners.'

That is the meaning of Calvary.

I WILL NEVER BECOME **A CHRISTIAN**

● 3. The success of it

Christ died for sins *once for all*. It was a 'once-for-all' act. It was unrepeatable because it was a hundred per cent successful. This man 'offered for all time one sacrifice for sins' (*Hebrews* 10:12). The success was assured because it was planned by the omnipotent Sovereign God. Peter again made this abundantly clear in his sermon in *Acts* 2:23, 'This man was handed over to you by God's set purpose and foreknowledge.' When Jesus said on the cross 'It is finished' (*John* 19:30), he meant that everything necessary for the fulfilment of God's loving purpose was about to be accomplished in his death.

A. W. Pink tells the following story:

Some years ago a Christian farmer was deeply concerned over an unsaved carpenter. The farmer sought to set before his neighbour the Gospel of God's grace, and to explain how that the Finished Work of Christ was *sufficient* for his soul to rest upon. But the carpenter persisted in the belief that he must do something himself. One day the farmer asked the carpenter to make for him a gate, and when the gate was ready he carried it away in his wagon. He arranged for the carpenter to call on him the next morning and see the gate as it hung in the field. At the appointed hour the carpenter arrived and was surprised to find the farmer standing by with a sharp axe in his hand. 'What are you going to do?' he asked. 'I am going to add a few cuts and strokes to your work' was the response. 'But there is no need for it,' replied the carpenter, 'the gate is alright as it is. I did all that was necessary to it.' The farmer took no notice, but lifting his axe he slashed and hacked at the gate until it was completely spoiled. 'Look what you have done!' cried the carpenter. 'You have *ruined my work*!'

'Yes,' said the farmer, 'and that is exactly what you are trying to do. You are seeking to nullify the Finished Work of Christ by your own miserable additions to it!' God used this forceful object lesson to show the carpenter his mistake, and he was led to cast himself by faith upon what Christ had done for sinners. Reader, will *you* do the same?

● 4. The purpose of it

The purpose was *to bring you to God*. God's love made Calvary possible, but it was God's holiness that made it necessary. The problem has always been human sin, which separates man from God. Because of sin man is an enemy of God. He is not welcome in the presence of God. He is unacceptable, far away in nature, attitude, behaviour and desire.

God and man are as different as holiness and sin. They are completely incompatible, and that will continue unless sin is dealt with, and the sinner changed.

Sin, eventually, would bring you to God, but only condemned and set for hell. The aim of the gospel is to bring man to God acceptable and righteous. This is an immense task, and the only way to accomplish this is the way of the cross. By his death on the cross Jesus dealt with:

the guilt of sin—he took it upon himself;

the wrath of God—he became the object of God's holy wrath for us, appeasing divine justice;

the corruption of man—he made it possible for God to remain just and yet exonerate sinners (*Romans* 3:26).

Faith in what Jesus has done credits us, in spite of our sin, with the righteousness of Jesus. All this is possible only because Christ died. He brings us to God.

A CHRISTIAN IS SOMEONE WHO HAS RESPONDED
TO THE GOSPEL IN THE WAY THAT GOD DEMANDS

In *John* 3:16 Jesus says that if we are not to perish our response must be to believe in him as Saviour. In the New Testament, to believe means more than acknowledging the truth of certain facts. It means to act in a way consistent with what we believe. If we believe we are sinners and can do nothing about that sin, and we also believe that God has done all that is necessary, we will act upon our belief and repent of the sin and come to Jesus for forgiveness. It is interesting that Jesus puts these two things together in *Mark* 1:15, '"The time has come," he said. "The kingdom of God is near. Repent and believe the good news!"'

Repentance means more than feeling sorry for your sin. You can be sorry for the consequences of sin, for being caught out, without having the slightest sense of guilt and sorrow for what you have done. Repentance means to want to be done with sin and to cry to God for mercy and pardon.

With repentance there will be belief or faith in Jesus, that in him God forgives all sin. This is the only way to become a Christian. However, salvation is more than forgiveness of sin. Thank God there is forgiveness for guilty sinners, but the gospel offers us more than that.

It is not unusual from time to time to hear that the ruler of a country on some great national occasion offers an amnesty to certain convicted criminals. Their sentences are quashed and they are set free. That is not an everyday occurrence but it is not unheard of. What is never heard of is a king or queen, after granting an amnesty, standing at the gates of the gaol to welcome the forgiven criminals as they come to freedom, and then telling them that as well as being released they are to come and live at the royal palace where they will be treated as members of the family. The love and care shown within the family will now be shown to them.

We never hear of that, and it is so improbable that it seems ridiculous even to think of it. But that is exactly what God does when he saves guilty sinners. He pardons all their sin, past, present, and future; but more than that—he adopts them into his family. He makes them joint-heirs with Christ of all the riches of heaven. He becomes their Father and because of this adoption they are able to call him Father.

That is the glorious salvation that we have in the Lord Jesus Christ. It is far, far more than forgiveness.

3 BECOMING A CHRISTIAN

We have been considering biblical Christianity, not
the hundred and one different varieties of
the original on offer today. Perhaps your
determination never to become a Christian
is because you have never before realized
what Christianity is.

○ Do you want to reject a Saviour who loved you so much that he
faced the judgement of God instead of you and died for you?
○ Do you want to reject a God who loved you so much that he
planned and arranged for his Son to do this for you?
○ Do you want to reject your only hope of forgiveness of sins and
your chance to start all over again?

HOW CAN YOU BECOME A CHRISTIAN?

By first of all realizing that you *need* to become a Christian, and that
this is the greatest need of your life. You have this need because you
are a sinner, and your sin not only separates you from God now but it
will do so for all eternity unless it is removed. You cannot deal with it.
Only God can do this. Remember there are only two places where

God deals with sin. One is on the cross of Calvary. The other is in hell. Like every human being your sin will be dealt with in one of those two places. At the cross it can be forgiven; in hell it for ever receives the judgement of God.

If you know you are a sinner and that, left to yourself, you have no hope, there is only one reasonable thing to do. Flee to Jesus who is your only hope. In other words, there is a sense of urgency about this. Becoming a Christian cannot be a casual act. If your attitude is, 'I'll give it a try to see if it works', then you still do not see the real need you have. You still do not appreciate that Jesus is the only Saviour. Becoming a Christian is not an experiment. It is an act of extreme urgency and desperation. The drowning man does not say to the lifeguard, 'Thank you for your interest in me and your offer of help. I'll consider your proposition and let you know my answer.' The situation in which he finds himself does not allow for the luxury of dithering. Neither does the situation of the sinner. The matter is urgent.

You *must* become a Christian.

You *must* be saved from the consequences of your sin.

You *must* come to Jesus for salvation.

You must also realize that you cannot become a Christian any time you choose. Jesus spells it out very clearly in *John* 6:44—'No one can come to me unless the Father who sent me draws him.'

If you really were determined never to become a Christian, then merely reading this book or any other book would not change your mind. It takes more than human argument and persuasion. It takes the drawing power of God. This means that God begins to soften the heart and make it receptive to the gospel. God may use a sermon, a book, the testimony of a friend, circumstances, or some other means in drawing you; but the result is that the gospel begins to have an effect. You find yourself thinking about spiritual things, whereas previously you never did. It may be you argue more strongly against Christianity than ever, but you are not so sure as you once were that it is all rubbish. Without this activity of God in your heart and mind you would be as determined as ever never to become a Christian.

Is God drawing you? If so, then come to Jesus with the assurance that Jesus gives: 'Whoever comes to me I will never drive away' (*John* 6:37). When you come to Jesus you will find that Christianity is not merely an insurance policy against punishment for sin; it opens to you a new life in the Saviour that you could not imagine. But first you must come in repentance and faith to the only one who can forgive your sins.

DO YOU WANT TO BE A CHRISTIAN?

If so, then it must be on God's terms. You cannot negotiate with the Almighty. His terms are these:

❍ Jesus Christ is the only Saviour.

❍ You must repent, that is, turn from your sin to Christ. Repentance does not mean you try your best to give up sinning. It means you acknowledge your bondage to sin and ask Jesus to set you free.

❍ You must have faith in the Lord Jesus Christ. Saving faith always includes three elements:

knowledge of the truth.

belief in that truth.

acting on that belief and coming to Jesus Christ.

To come to Jesus means to believe in Jesus, that is to believe who he is and what he has done to make sinners acceptable to God. It means to trust Jesus, to commit your life to him, and to ask him to forgive you your sins. Then, having come to the Lord Jesus Christ in repentance and faith, you live a new way of life according to his standards.

In 1979 I was preaching at the West of England Festival of Male Voice Praise in the Colston Hall, Bristol. These are always very popular occasions and two thousand people filled the Hall. After the meeting the road outside was packed with coaches and cars picking up these two thousand folk as well as those coming from theatres that were pouring out their audiences at the same time. The traffic was so thick that nothing was moving. We were parked behind the Colston Hall, on the fifth floor of an eleven-storey car park. Because of the traffic jam in the road no cars could leave the car park. The ramps connecting the floors were also solid with traffic, right up to where we were parked.

It appeared as if we would be there for hours, but one of the passengers with us knew Bristol well from his student days and he said, 'There is no need to go down; go up. There is an exit on the eighth floor.' We thought he was joking. Who had ever heard of an exit on the eighth floor? But we had nothing to lose, so we followed the strange advice. Everyone else was trying to go down and ours was the only car going up. To our amazement he was right. There was an exit on the eighth floor. Apparently this is possible because the car park is built against the side of a hill. In no time at all we were out and on our way home. The obvious way was to go down, and everyone took it, but someone knew another way. Go up, he said;

and it worked. We obeyed and were free of the mess in which everyone else remained.

Which way are you going with your life? The Bible says, 'There is a way that seems right to a man, but in the end it leads to death' (*Proverbs* 14:12). There is another way. It is not our way. It is God's way. Jesus said, 'I am the way' (*John* 14:6). The only way home to God out of the mess of sin is through the Lord Jesus Christ.

4 I AM A CHRISTIAN

What we have been considering is not empty speculation, but what millions of people from all types of backgrounds have found to be complete reality. Read now the testimonies of some ordinary men and women.

A CARPENTER—THOUGHT CHRISTIANS WERE ANNOYING, UNTIL HE READ THE BIBLE FOR HIMSELF

I became a Christian at the age of nineteen. Of all people I would have been the last that anyone would expect to become a Christian. People sometimes say about Christians, 'Well, if you are that way inclined, OK but personally I am not.' The truth is, neither was I 'that way inclined'. My father had always brought me up to believe that there was no God, and that was fine with me. Until I was nineteen I do not think that I had known a Christian, or at least one who stood up for his faith. I had had the odd encounter on the street or at the front door with some Christians, but basically to me and my friends they were either an annoyance or objects of ridicule. At school I was given a New Testament which I began to read. The problem was that I did not understand it and nobody could explain it to me, so after a while I stopped trying.

I WILL NEVER BECOME **A CHRISTIAN**

When I left school I became a carpenter and joiner and thought that I was really enjoying life. Most of my evenings were spent in pubs, clubs, and discos. In fact, it got to the stage where I could not stay in, thinking that I might miss a 'good night out'. Then one day, my father and mother went to church, having been introduced by an uncle and aunt. This was a surprise in itself because he was such a convinced atheist. What was even more surprising was that within a very short time my father was converted. I could not understand what had happened to him. He started to read the Bible and talked to me about it. I was amazed and decided to find out for myself what had changed him. It was not that I believed what he told me—in fact for some time I tried to prove him wrong. Eventually I went to church and found that the Bible, which I had attempted to read five years previously, was being explained, and not only that but that it was relevant for today. I began to read it again and things started to make sense. I found out what I was really like inside and how I needed cleansing and forgiveness from God. But I also understood, for the first time in my life, that the cleansing and forgiveness I needed were what Jesus had died for on the cross. All I needed was in him and it was all free. When I asked for forgiveness I received it, just as he promises to all who come to him in repentance and faith.

From then on I had a new desire in my life: to live for him and to know more and more of him. My sisters thought it was a shame and a waste of my life. To me it was the best thing that ever happened. Since then they have become Christians and now agree with me. Living a Christian life anywhere is a battle, no less so on a building site. When I was first converted my foreman said that I would be back 'with the lads' within three months. That was over eight years ago and my Christian faith now is stronger than ever. Although it has not always been easy, it has been good, and by the grace and enabling of God I will continue to the end.

A HOUSEWIFE—SERVING GOD IN THE HOME AND FAMILY

'… for better for worse, for richer for poorer, in sickness and in health …'

I remember hearing those words on that special day twenty-five years ago when I was married. It was then that I embarked on a career in homemaking with all its ups and downs. At times I wondered if I could possibly cope; but, for me, functioning as a housewife is definitely linked with my being a Christian.

I was converted at the age of fifteen. God wonderfully intervened in my life as I searched to discover what life was all about and why I was made. I realized that there would be a cost involved in being a disciple of Christ, but I was determined to follow him. I committed myself to doing all things to the best of my ability as I wished to bring glory to God's name. This included my role as a wife. Suddenly, I was no longer independent, I was to be a helper to my husband in a permanent, mutually supportive partnership in which neither was in servitude to the other.

With the birth of our first child, I was given the additional role of mother with its extra demands and responsibilities. The pressure was only to increase in subsequent years with two further additions to the family unit. I discovered that beautiful babies scream at night; that they suffer from colic; that they do not follow the patterns of sleep or feeding that we would desire. I knew what it was to be exhausted, but was convinced that the children came first and the family had to be fitted around the children's needs. As I fed and clothed them, and provided security and affection, I was constantly aware of the fact that I was the most formative influence in their lives. Thus, I was to train and discipline them so that they might develop into happy, well-adjusted adults, but what a task! Yet, my greatest desire was to teach my children about God. Often it was quite a strain to get the three ready for church on time, and then there was still the question of keeping them quiet during the service. In these years I learned the truth of these words of the Bible: 'Cast all your anxiety on him [God] because he cares for you' (*1 Peter* 5:7).

Frequently I have known God injecting his energy when I was drained and ready to drop. There have been times when, with the bedtime stories ended, I have crept downstairs for a hard-earned moment of relaxation thinking the children were all asleep, only to be called back upstairs by the cry of one of them. All mothers know this, but during these stressful times it is certainly a great privilege to be able to cry to God, knowing that he hears and cares. He is my caring heavenly Father.

Each stage of motherhood requires development of a particular area of one's character. I think that patience is the vital ingredient in the teenage years. At times I felt like exploding, and sometimes did, as I viewed the chaos in the bedrooms and I had to learn to cope with the house becoming something akin to Clapham Junction station, as friends sped in and out. Then there is the wisdom and sensitivity needed to advise on sex and drugs, on alcohol and entertainment. Often I have wanted to run away, feeling I have failed, as I have reflected on a wrong response to a situation. I am so thankful that I can turn to my perfect heavenly Father, who loves me despite my failings and can, in his sovereign power, use even my mistakes to accomplish his purposes.

God does not expect me to be a perfect housewife, but he does expect me to be the best I can be. He expects me to utilize all my God-given gifts and abilities to fulfil my potential for his glory. To be fully employed as a housewife and mother is in no way a waste of a woman's abilities, as far as I am concerned, but rather a test of them. As I seek to do my best for God's glory, I can trust that my family are safe in his hands. From experience I can say, 'Thus far has the Lord helped me.' How could I continue one step without his help?

A MINER—A TOUGH MAN OF THE WORLD
DRAWN IRRESISTIBLY TO CHRIST

I got off to a bad start as both my parents were godless. I went to work down the pits straight from school and have done the same job for forty-five years. It is a hard life down the mines: working in dark, damp, cramped and dangerous conditions breeds tough men whose soft hearts are hidden in the bravado of heavy drinking, betting and swearing. I am not making excuses for myself. Like the rest I worked hard down there for as much money as I could get—'If there's nowt goes into t'empty [tub] there's nowt goes into t'tin [wages].' All this for gambling, smoking, drinking—and how I loved these sessions! My wife and seven children came last. Often when I had spent up I would look at myself in the mirror and say, 'Never no more', but each time I reverted to my old ways. This went on for years. You can imagine what my marriage was like. Both my wife and I hit rock-bottom many times—but she kept on forgiving me. I was one of the most unlikely people to consider becoming a Christian, but God had different ideas. First he brought me into an evangelical church.

When my wife's sister died we went to an evangelical church for the funeral. Up till then I thought it had been turned into a storehouse, but I soon found out differently. The minister came to the house and we said we would come again. For some reason I found myself wanting to go to church on the next Sunday evening—I do not know why as I had only gone through a church door at weddings and funerals before. We kept on going, drawn mainly by the friendship and kindness the people there showed us. At times we thought we would not go again. I used to say, 'I hope he doesn't preach that awful sin again.' It really did hurt us. We thought that maybe he would not the next time and so we carried on.

Then my wife became a Christian. She went to a prayer-meeting one night when I was at work, and the next morning I found she was a different person to look at and to listen to. I could see the radiance and happiness in her face, and it seemed a remarkable achievement to me that somebody ordinary could be like that. It made me study a lot but I thought, 'I'm all right as I am.'

That is when my fight really started. I became annoyed at the minister because I thought he knew all about my personal life and was getting at me in his sermons, but I kept on going to the church with my wife. Many times I was moved to tears, each time vowing I was never going again. But, to my surprise, come the next Sunday I was first to be ready. I felt confused and angry inside. At work I was like an old bear; I was grumpy and sometimes nasty with my workmates, and I even turned on my wife. I knew something was wrong. I spent hours worrying about it and I could not sleep at nights. At last I decided I had to go to the source of my trouble—the minister. I told him there was something wrong with me, I could not rest, it was all his fault, and he had to put it right! He told me I had to take it to the Lord, so together with my wife we went into the church and prayed. I asked God to empty my heart of sin. Often I had sung the words

Foul, I to the fountain fly;
Wash me, Saviour, or I die.

This time he did. All that filth emptied from me and I felt different. My hardened heart was melted, Jesus came into my life, and I was born again. It took me some time to grasp that the minister had been just doing his job and that it was God who had saved me. He was the one who had been pointing at me and breaking down my pride until I admitted my need of him. That night when I left the church it was like walking on a cushion of air.

Soon afterwards the Lord helped me to break with my old habits. This was not always easy. When I was bursting for a drink I would put my head under the tap and fill the sink up to the top with water. I stopped cursing and swearing and felt completely changed. It was the beginning.

The next step was to make a Christian stand down the pit, and I had no doubts about the ridicule I would have to put up with. Working in danger, with men you have known all your life, makes you one of the team, known and accepted. Now I was different and they were dead set against it. They played all kinds of unpleasant tricks to make me crack. They would trip me up in the mud and shout, 'He is praying again. Say one for me, Arthur.' Other times things would come flying at me from the darkness or they would flash their lights in my eyes to make me drop things and hurt myself—all to make me lose control and swear. By the grace of God they missed out. I took it all and just kept on working. Bit by bit they began to respect me for my beliefs.

People said my conversion was a nine days' wonder, but it is twelve years since I died to that old, sinful life. Some days the devil still comes roaring like a lion, but by his grace the Lord has given me power to resist temptations. The artificial pleasures of the world are meaningless to me now; I have left them all behind for my Lord. Now I work for him, particularly in old people's homes.

I still keep a photograph of myself which carries the look of a condemned man. If I had continued in my old life I think I would have been 'pushing up daisies' by now. Instead I am living proof that God's power has changed me and kept me.

A DOCTOR—FROM INDIFFERENCE TO THE GOSPEL, TO SEEING THE POWER OF GOD AT WORK IN HIS LIFE AND THAT OF OTHERS

Many who have been awakened by the power of the Holy Spirit to consider the state of their souls, their standing before God, and their need to be converted, are often concerned about such questions as 'Will I be able to maintain a good Christian life?' or 'Will I be able to live up to the Christian standards?' The twenty-eight years of my Christian life testify to God's keeping power and grace.

I was converted at the age of twenty-one and really did not give much thought or attention to religious matters before this. Like most youngsters in Wales in those days, I had gone to Sunday School and chapel until about the age of twelve or thirteen, but I was not really interested in the gospel. In fact, I do not think that I had ever heard the gospel preached in the local chapel. I left home at the age of seventeen and went to medical school in London, but it was not until four years into the course that I met a group of evangelical believers who were obviously different and proved to be good, wholesome people whose company I liked. I became very friendly with them and eventually one of them invited me to church. I was to meet him at St James's Park underground station in London, but he did not turn up. The chapel was just around the corner and so I made my way there with my girlfriend—just a little late. There was hardly a seat to be found and we were tucked into two seats right at the back, just as the preacher was going up into the pulpit. He began to pray and I was aware instantly of a feeling which I had never experienced before in other religious services. There was an urgency, there was a seriousness, there was a sense that the matters being prayed about and which were to be considered were the most important and momentous that could ever be considered by anyone. It was over the next six to eight weeks that I was converted.

The first three or four years of my Christian life saw me troubled very much as to whether I was really right with God. I began seeking God more. The job that I had at that time was in a hospital in London. Although it was not a busy job, I found myself confined to the mess in the evenings with little to do. This was a blessing, in that I had an abundance of time to seek the Lord.

All Christians witness to the power of God to keep them despite their own unworthiness, and my testimony would be no exception to this general rule. I bless God for many of the experiences which I have had. One is that for ten years I was lay pastor of a small group of Christians back in my home town, and in that context I saw the problems and difficulties that Christians experience in a very different light from that in which I saw them in a professional role. This was invaluable, and it taught me much of the kind of burdens that ministers bear in their pastoral capacities that I would not have known otherwise. I have also known the keeping power of God in my professional work in the Health Service. Many people in the UK are disillusioned with the Health Service (whatever government may be in power). One of my problems is that as a Christian I wish to speak to people, patients and others, about the Lord Jesus Christ, but the busyness of the Health Service makes this impossible. My conclusion is that one can only attempt to be sensitive to the Spirit, and through his leadings seek to help the comparatively small number who perhaps have spiritual problems and with whom God is dealing.

Some years ago I saw a young lady who had difficulty in walking. She had been investigated thoroughly but no physical cause was found for her problems. Assessment of her situation indicated that she was very unhappy indeed. She had become forlorn and isolated, and her marriage had broken up. Her problems led to great stress.

Conversation concerning the things of God indicated little interest and she was desperately lonely. With her agreement I wrote to the pastor of her local church, and the church befriended her. To my great joy, when I saw her some three months later, not only was she 'cured' from the psychiatric point of view, but she had been saved.

A COMPANY DIRECTOR—RESCUED BY GOD FROM REBELLION, AND DAILY NEEDING GOD'S HELP TO COPE WITH PRESSURE AT WORK

Mine was not a sudden conversion, one that can be identified within close and well-defined limits. Having drifted away from Sunday School and church attendance during my youth I was invited with my wife to a Sunday evening Presbyterian Church service some thirty or so years ago. Attendance followed more or less regularly until we both were taken into church membership about two years later.

There followed a period of growing involvement in church life and the Lord's work through Sunday School teaching and leadership. Accompanying this involvement was a growing awareness of the fulness of Christ's gospel in terms of its saving consequences and its demands on the life of the believer. It was about five years after attending that first meeting that I can now identify as a period of change from nominal church membership, through busy activity, to a full realization of God's sovereign grace in salvation through Jesus Christ, and of my dependence on him for my daily needs.

I was brought up by a Christian mother in a non-Christian home, was taught to respect God, his Word, and the Sabbath, and was shown the need for the saving work of Jesus Christ in the hearts of unbelievers. I was made to attend Sunday School and church services, generally against my will and with a growing rebellion. The attractions of the world were far more important than things spiritual and eternal, and I thought that there was plenty of time before needing to think seriously and decisively about my soul and its future in eternity.

Looking back I can now trace God's hand throughout my life. His working through early teaching in the Scriptures proved invaluable.

His leading to and through specific circumstances, which previously I had considered the random happenings of life, I now see clearly as part of his divine purpose for me. Gone are the days when I thought that I could live without Christ's saving power and his strength and wisdom to sustain me in my daily living.

I now realize my own helplessness outside his grace, and am constrained to call on him daily for guidance in facing the responsibilities of the day and in the inevitable decisions that have to be made. Such decisions not only have to be correct and for the good of the company, but also have to take into account the interests and concerns of the employees who make up the company. They are decisions that have to be made not only with business expediency in mind but also with the honesty and integrity demanded of the Christian.

Daily I need to cast myself on God for strength to withstand the pressures of the job: the long hours and frequent travel, the demanding workload, and the need to achieve the trading results essential for a healthy company. I also need strength to bear the occasional feeling of loneliness which accompanies unpalatable, but nevertheless necessary, decisions which personally affect individual employees. 'Even there your hand will guide me, your right hand will hold me fast', says the psalmist (139:10). The reality of God's leading and protection is now my strength and assurance in facing the problems of the day: strength in the knowledge that I am not alone, and that when things appear to be going all wrong God is in control; assurance in the knowledge that when things turn out differently from the way I had wished, he is doing what is right for me, for 'his way is perfect' (*Psalm* 18:30).

A UNIVERSITY LECTURER—TRUSTING IN THE TRUTH
OF THE BIBLE IN THE FACE OF INTELLECTUAL ATTACK

When I was studying at Imperial College, London, I happened to read a comment column in a national paper. It recommended that creationists should 'press their noses' against some of the exhibits in the Natural History Museum to become convinced about evolution. I wrote to the paper informing them that I studied not 200 metres from those exhibits, and never considered pressing my nose against them. I might have added that Sherlock Holmes did not stoop to pressing his nose to the evidence, and yet who besides him could solve the crime? Now that I am at Cambridge, I can count among my friends a leading Darwinian and author on the subject.

Science of course is interested in truth not dogma, and to find truth it proposes theories, which are then supported or attacked. I am quite happy to reject evolution in favour of creation because I hold some extra evidence, namely that of God's Word, and I have that gift of God that is faith to 'understand that the universe was formed at God's command, so that what is seen was not made out of what was visible' (*Hebrews* 11:3). Looking at the visible facts one aligns them, including examples of observable evolution, with creation. This is not at all hard, especially given that God is almighty.

Belief in Almighty God leads one to trust the Bible as the only written revelation of God, and in it we find the truth about ourselves. Are we people who are just a little bit weak in some respect? Or are we superstitiously in need of a few good deeds to ensure a good life, now and hereafter? Are we just emotional wrecks and failures at life? I am none of these. I am a hard-headed engineer, lecturer, and company director. However, the Bible says that I was 'dead in [my] transgressions and sins' (*Ephesians* 2:1). When I first heard that, I knew it to be true. I was not weak or feeble, I was dead! The good news of God in the Bible is that Christ saves those who admit their sin and deadness to him, and who look to him alone for life.

Since hearing that for the first time, I have been trusting Christ for forgiveness of sins, and he has given me new life. By that, I mean a life in which I know God to be the King of kings and Lord of lords, who loves me and cares about me. I have his words to guide me and encourage me, and his Spirit in me to help me understand his Word, myself, and the world. Every aspect of life has another dimension, one for which we were created but which we forfeited because of sin. Without it we have a lingering death: with it we have true life, with real meaning. I would rather have life.

A BLACK SOUTH AFRICAN—ONCE DETERMINED NEVER TO BECOME A CHRISTIAN, NOW REJOICING IN CHRIST

'There are many devices in the heart of a man; but the counsel of the Lord, that shall stand.'

As a young black South African at high school in the eighties I vowed never to become a Christian. This was occasioned by a socio-economic and political setting, and the related perception that Christianity was a European tool to expropriate the indigenous people and make them subservient and dependent on the whites. As it has been put,

When the white men came, we had the land and they had the

Bible. They taught us to pray with our eyes shut. When we opened our eyes, they had the land and we had the Bible!

Also the radical change of lifestyle involved in being born again threatened the very core of our definition of fun and pleasure. As a young man experimenting and deriving pleasure from all sorts of forbidden things, I could never look favourably on Christianity. I loved and enjoyed the things I was doing. Christianity was not just challenging these but positively disapproved of them, and that enraged me. I vowed never to become a Christian.

The perception that being a Christian implies intellectual weakness and brainwashing by the white man's religion bolstered my determination to resist. As if this was not enough, I and my friends seized opportunities in open debates to ridicule, taunt and pull down Christians as being unreasonable and even intellectually challenged. It seemed we won most of these debates; some Christians would leave crying, and promising to ask their God to save us. We thought they were crazy, but over ten years later I met one of them again and was able to tell her that God had heard her prayer!

Before I left school things began to change. The man in darkness, the lover of pleasures, was faced with difficulties ranging from physical danger to intense spiritual problems. Help was desperately needed. I tried various avenues for this, including consulting a spiritist medium; I soon discarded the paraphernalia that she gave me. I cried much to God, though without invoking the name of Christ, to which I still had an aversion as being the white man's Saviour.

One evening I was returning from time out drinking with friends when I saw a church building all lit up. For some unknown reason I was drawn to go in. I took leave of my friends and went in, still with a completely negative attitude, ready to criticize everything I heard. At the end I learned that there would be further meetings each day for the next three weeks, in preparation for a prolonged outreach in the neighbouring township. Despite my continuing drink and drugs-fuelled lifestyle, I found myself going back to this church for every one of those meetings. There I was exposed to the gospel being preached by a man from Swaziland. I was probably the only unbeliever there.

One evening he took for his text *Isaiah* 43:25; 'I, even I, am he who blots out your transgressions, for my own sake, and remembers your sins no more.' At the end he invited those who wanted to be saved to raise their hands. I did so, and was taken aside for counselling. But the thought of joining these Christians repelled me, and I summarily took my leave, determined not to come back.

For two days I held out against the idea of becoming a Christian. On the third day I went up a mountain and there confessed all my sins to God and cried to him to forgive me. When I came down from that mountain I knew that I was truly a brand new man. Oh happy day when God saved me, forgave my sins and granted me a fresh start! I discovered that one can truly be joyful and at peace without partaking of the things I used to think were the only source of happiness. In Christ I found love, acceptance, a new identity and indeed a whole new life.

Since those early days, the Lord has dealt remarkably with me. He has led me into marriage, having a family, Christian service, and I am now pastor of a small church in England.

So much for my vow never to become a Christian!

A JEWISH WOMAN—FOUND LIFE EMPTY AND
MEANINGLESS, UNTIL SHE CAME TO CHRIST

My journey, one which was to take me to many parts of the world, began when I was thirteen and starting to notice that there was something missing in my life! Surely you don't just go to school, go home, do your homework and play. I came from a very secular Israeli home but I began to look for some spiritual input to my life. I looked at the fanatical Orthodox Jews who walked around the neighbourhood but they didn't seem spiritual, just kind of scary. So I bought an expensive book about Transcendental Meditation and I remember thinking: Why does it cost so much money to get to happiness? I examined many different cults, got involved in Tarot reading and New Age teaching but I was still looking for God. I always found that what people taught me was a big lie. Everyone wanted something from me. Either they wanted my money, to take advantage of me, or to brainwash me. I knew the Bible was real but in Israel it is taught from a secular point of view. So my life was really turbulent.

I had great grades in school, but that didn't interest me, so I left school. I then worked as a sales person and made lots of money, but that didn't interest me either. I always had friends around me and we went to parties and had a good time, but that didn't interest me, so I found new friends (I changed all my friends every six months!). It was like I had everything, but I didn't want it. At some point I knew I had to leave Israel. I felt I was just dying. I started to travel the world and it was in Japan that I came to an end of myself.

In Japan most people seemed to be in pursuit of money all the time. I made big money there but threw it all away gambling and partying. One day I thought, 'OK, let's check out Shinto.' I sat down under a lovely tree beside a colourful temple in a beautiful garden, watched the monks walking really slowly, and listened as they banged a gong. I went to meditate because I had been so shocked by all the materialism I had seen. Suddenly something hit me from behind and I realized it was a big insect. The trees were full of those insects and as I looked at them I noticed a sign declaring that the shrine was dedicated to that type of insect. I said to myself, 'How low can you get! How can you worship an insect?'

From that point, my life started to go downhill but I had a drug addiction and didn't care where I was going. I didn't even want to hold on to the thought that maybe I would one day find God. I went back to Israel but I didn't find myself there. I wanted to go to Africa, but I couldn't get there. Finally I went to Portugal and started selling oil paintings. I didn't care about money and didn't care about myself. If there was no chance of me communicating with God, I didn't see any point in living.

But then one day, by chance, it seemed, I came to England. I started selling oil paintings, moving from apartment to apartment and going from job to job. I was really reaching the end. I had decided that this world had nothing to offer me. I had money, I had fun, I had men, I went to lots of parties, I travelled, but it was boring.

I decided I was going to kill myself but I was living next door to a 'Jesus freak' who told me about Jesus. That really made me mad: 'Yeah, you're going to tell me that God came down from the skies and did this and that!' As I was deciding which way I was going to kill myself, I told him to bring what I called his 'Messianic rabbi' to me. I wanted to listen to him before I killed myself because I had an inkling that there might be a hell and I didn't want to go there. So I met this man, who looked like a salesman to me. I thought he might have some sales tricks up his sleeve, so I said, 'What do you want to tell me? What's your claim? What is your cult into?'

I soon realized that he didn't want to take advantage of me in any way. 'OK,' I said, 'Why have you come to this crazy conclusion that God can die?' He opened a Hebrew Bible—the Bible that I had known from school—and verse by verse he showed me that the Messiah would be born of a woman and would suffer and die. That very day I accepted Yeshua and decided not to kill myself! When I went home, I was on cloud nine. I started to read the New Testament. It took me four months and I had many difficult questions: Why was Judas such a bad guy? Could I be Judas? Could I make one mistake too many? What if I had the Holy Spirit and I blasphemed—would I be doomed? I was really struggling with this huge idea, that God himself, the infinite, came into a body to die for me, the nobody. He really loved me and I was not a nice person. He forgives me! It's difficult to comprehend!

But I knew I had found reality for the first time in my life. I went back to Israel thinking that people would persecute me when I spoke of Yeshua but it didn't happen. Instead, a series of miracles happened. I found a huge congregation of believers in Eilat and I started evangelizing in the desert. I talked to people about God and they actually listened to me, listened to the Holy Spirit speaking through me. I saw two people come to the Lord during one month! I have now been baptized and am following a discipleship course.

I came to England from Portugal 'by chance' but God knew what he was doing!

I WILL NEVER BECOME **A CHRISTIAN**

If you should require any further help concerning the matters raised in this book or on any other aspect of Christian faith and life, contact the publisher.

QUOTATIONS

Quotations are taken from the following publications:

J. Edwin Orr, *The Flaming Tongue* (Moody Press).

Peter Masters, *Answers to Questions* (Wakeman Trust).

Marshall's Bible Handbook (Marshall, Morgan and Scott).

B.G. Ranganathan, *Origins?* (Banner of Truth Trust).

Time Magazine, December 1974.

James Montgomery Boice, *Foundations of the Christian Faith* (Inter-Varsity Press).

Herbert M. Carson, *Facing Suffering* (Evangelical Press).

Revival Digest, September 1989.

A.W. Pink, *Seven Sayings of the Saviour on the Cross* (Baker Book House).

I WILL NEVER BECOME **A CHRISTIAN**

I WILL NEVER BECOME **A CHRISTIAN**

I WILL NEVER BECOME **A CHRISTIAN**

I WILL NEVER BECOME **A CHRISTIAN**

HOW CAN GOD ACCEPT ME?

GERARD CHRISPIN

This attractive yet frank, God-centred, gospel presentation persuades readers to examine their lives afresh and to turn to Jesus Christ. With quality photo-illustrations throughout, it is suitable for: missions, church evangelism, open air meetings, visitation, youth, the student world, rest homes, hospitals and prisons.

'… an outstanding presentation of the gospel, concise, clear and biblical. It is a highly commendable tool to be used in personal evangelism.'
JOHN MACARTHUR

32PP, POCKET-SIZE BOOKLET
COLOUR THROUGHOUT
ISBN 1 903087 09 0

HOW CAN I FIND GOD?

GERARD CHRISPIN

'How can I find God?' like 'How can God accept me?' uses clear and uncluttered language, and makes a compelling presentation of the gospel. A must for evangelism!

16 PAGES POCKET-SIZE BOOKLET
COLOUR THROUGHOUT
ISBN 1 903087 53 8

HOW CAN I BECOME A REAL CHRISTIAN?

GERARD CHRISPIN

Very attractively presented pocket-sized booklet, with colour graphics, appropriate for all forms of evangelism.

'…simple, clear, yet thorough presentation of the gospel message.'
ALISTAIR BEGG

32PP POCKET SIZE-BOOKLET
COLOUR THROUGHOUT
ISBN 1 903087 93 7

Day One Publications Ryelands Road Leominster HR6 8NZ
email: sales@dayone.co.uk www.dayone.co.uk ☎ 01568 613 740

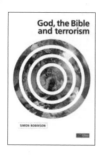

GOD, THE BIBLE AND TERRORISM

SIMON J ROBINSON

Since the events of July 7th and July 21st, terrorism in the UK has become much more than just a news item on TV. In this graphically illustrated booklet, Simon Robinson articulately addresses this important issue, considering points such as 'How would Jesus respond to the London bombings?', 'Is this God's judgement?', 'Forgiveness and justice' and 'Seeking the Lord while he may still be found'.

Simon Robinson is the senior minister of Walton Evangelical Church, Chesterfield. He has also written several other books, all published by Day One, and is editor of the new *Face2face with …* series.

'Simon challenges us to … look at our own lives and how we will respond to the Judge of all the Earth when our time inevitably comes to meet him.'
MARK MULLINS

Discounts for quantity purchases

16PP BOOKLET, ILLUSTRATED
COLOUR THROUGHOUT
ISBN 1 84625 017 X

OPENING UP EZEKIEL'S VISIONS

PETER JEFFERY

In a time of international confusion and individual uncertainty, nothing is better than clear thinking and clear, authoritative speaking. Such qualities were shown by God's prophet, Ezekiel, as he wrote to the confused and scattered people of God some eight centuries before Christ. What was the source of their grave personal and national problems? Was their situation beyond remedy and hope? Could anything be done? Where was God in all this? Does God personally intervene in the affairs of men and nations? All these questions and many more were addressed by Ezekiel—with God's authority as God's prophet to his people and the times.

Clearly written, with no punches pulled as far as contemporary application is concerned, this is just the sort of help needed by those who otherwise might find the book difficult to understand. Peter Jeffery has succeeded in bringing home to twenty-first century people God's ever relevant diagnosis of their condition and his remedy for it.'
GRAHAM HARRISON, MINISTER OF EMMANUEL CHAPEL, NEWPORT AND LECTURER IN CHRISTIAN DOCTRINE, LONDON THEOLOGICAL SEMINARY

128PP PAPERBACK
ISBN 1 903087 66 X

Day One Publications Ryelands Road Leominster HR6 8NZ
email: sales@dayone.co.uk www.dayone.co.uk ☎ 01568 613 740